A DEEP DIVE

An Expert Analysis of Police Procedure, Use of Force and Wrongful Convictions

Timothy T. Williams Jr.
CEO, T.T. Williams Jr., Investigations, Inc.

A Deep Dive: An Expert Analysis of Police Procedure, Use of Force and Wrongful Convictions

CEO, T.T. Williams Jr., Investigations, Inc.

Disclaimer:

The author strives to be as accurate and complete as possible in the creation of this book, notwithstanding the fact that the author does not warrant or represent at any time that the contents within are accurate due to the rapidly changing nature of the Internet.

While all attempts have been made to verify information provided in this publication, the Author and the Publisher assume no responsibility and are not liable for errors, omissions, or contrary interpretation of the subject matter herein. The Author and Publisher hereby disclaim any liability, loss or damage incurred as a result of the application and utilization, whether directly or indirectly, of any information, suggestion, advice, or procedure in this book. Any perceived slights of specific persons, peoples, or organizations are unintentional.

In practical advice books, like anything else in life, there are no guarantees of income made. Readers are cautioned to rely on their own judgment about their individual circumstances to act accordingly. Readers are responsible for their own actions, choices, and results. This book is not intended for use as a source of legal, business, accounting or financial advice. All readers are advised to seek the services of competent professionals in legal, business, accounting, and finance field.

Printed in the United States of America

Photo Credit: David Grisham - DMG Imaging

Jones Media Publishing
www.jonesmediapublishing.com

ISBN: 978-1-945849-94-7 paperback
JMP2020.5

DEDICATION

THIS BOOK IS dedicated to my family who will always be with me through the good times and the bad times. They have withstood the test of time and my temperament.

First, I dedicate this, my first book, to my loving wife, Donna, who has been with me and supported me through this journey. She has kept me focused and ensured that I stay grounded, not losing sight of my goals and objectives. As you read the section of this book on court and deposition dress attire, she has been a major influence on me in that area. I would not have been able to experience my successes without her, and for that I love her dearly.

I dedicate this book to my late parents, my father Timothy, Sr. and my mother Glenn. My mother and father instilled in me my core values that are still in place today. They raised me and my siblings to stand tall with our head high, stand for right and address the wrong, and as my father always said, "Be up-front and down-front". My mother and father etched in my and my sibling's DNA as we were coming up, "Never let anyone tell you what you cannot do in life." I thank my parents for teaching me the lessons of life and for providing me with the tools to address the issues of life.

I dedicate this book to our children and their families, along with our grandchildren. They keep me doing what I do at the level I do it at, and I love them dearly. Our children and grandchildren are everything to us, and they will be left with a legacy to make a difference in a system that will mitigate the negative impact upon them and future generations of our family.

I dedicate this book to my siblings, Colbert, Sr., Gerald, my sister Frieda (and her husband Alfred), and my late brother, Selwyn. As the eldest sibling, I am always "Big Brother". They have put up with me all of their lives and I love them dearly. We talk several times a week and have always stayed close. I thank them for their support in all my endeavors in life and even on this new journey.

And finally, I dedicate this book to my nephews, niece, great-nephews, and my cousins from coast to coast in the United States, in Canada, Barbados, and Trinidad. We have been a major influence on each other's lives, just as those family members who came before us have been a major influence on our lives as it relates to tradition and core values. To my family, I thank you for your support and love.

CONTENTS

ACKNOWLEDGEMENTS

I WOULD LIKE TO acknowledge my administrative assistant, Joan, who keeps my office running like a fine-tuned engine. I thank her for her editorial recommendations as she reviewed portions of this book. She makes sure I get up from behind my desk and eat my lunch on a daily basis, and for that I am grateful.

I would like to acknowledge my web designer, Alexis, who designed my web page giving me a worldwide platform in my areas of expertise. Her work has generated many clients that have enhanced my practice, and for her professional creativity in my online presence, I am forever grateful.

I would also like to thank my publisher, Jones Media Publishing, who worked diligently with me on this, my first journey of being an author. It was a journey I will do again.

And finally, to my public relations firm, WrightOne Communications. They have kept me on track and managed me well.

"Our lives begin to end the day we become silent about things that matter."

Martin Luther King, Jr.

CHAPTER 1

THE BEGINNING AND THE DEFINITION

THE REASON I wrote this book is to give an accurate accounting and deep dive into what a Police Procedure, Use of Force, and Wrongful Conviction expert does from being retained as an expert in these areas through deposition and trial testimony. This book is designed not only for the general public but for attorneys, law students, media, and judges who render rulings in these matters.

In my lectures in the areas of my expertise, I cover the basic questions that I have been asked over the years. Hopefully you, the reader, will have your questions answered as I take you on a journey in my world. Before we begin this journey, I must give you a brief rundown as to my background. I am a retired Senior Detective Supervisor from the Los Angeles Police Department (LAPD) last assigned to the elite Robbery-Homicide Division. Of my over twenty-nine years working for LAPD, which began in May 1974, I dedicated over twenty-six years of my career to conducting criminal and administrative investigations along with working investigative and administrative assignments.

Prior to my retirement, I opened my practice, T. T. Williams, Jr., Investigations, Inc., doing civil investigations. Upon my retirement in October 2003, I included criminal investigations. Early in my practice upon my retirement, my jury trial testimony was focused on Police Procedure issues and nothing else. Based upon what I was being retained to do as it related to my trial testimony, I wrote a proposal requesting the creation of a Police Procedure Expert for the Los Angeles County Superior Court Expert Witness List. My request was approved and I was the only Police Procedure Expert on the Los Angeles County Superior Court Expert Witness List for approximately five years. I am a Police Procedure, Use of Force, and Wrongful Conviction Expert in both State and Federal Court, with active and prior cases in different parts of the country.

Let us begin this journey with defining what an expert is and is not. An expert is a teacher. A competent expert will level the playing field so the trier of fact, the jury in a jury trial or a judge in a court trial, can make informed decisions. An expert must have the qualifications, experience, and expertise to explain complex issues in both oral and written communication to the court and the jury. An expert opinion and testimony must meet industry standards and be supported by policy and procedure. Further, an expert must stay current in their craft to withstand the questioning of opposing counsel, the scrutiny of the court, and be able to defend their written report(s). An expert is not an advocate, but a neutral in the matter they are retained on. Their written report(s) should be based on industry standards and supported by written policy and procedure and not of written advocacy.

Testimony must also be based upon industry standards and supported by written policy and procedures. Taking the position of an advocate will ruin your credibility as an Expert Witness and will shorten the expert's career. Advocacy has its place, but not in the arena of Expert Witness work. I strongly encourage current Expert Witnesses and those who want to get into the Expert Witness work, if they are on the social media platform like Facebook, Instagram, Blogs, and Twitter to name a few, do not come across as an advocate. Social media platforms that some Expert Witnesses are active on have been and will be checked by opposing counsel in both criminal and civil cases. Controversial statements, views, and positions can and will end up in court and destroy the credibility of an Expert Witness. I have had experts approach me at the conclusion of my lectures trying to justify why they have an active presence on these social platforms, and my response has been, "A word to the wise should be sufficient."

Now that an expert has been defined, let's look at what I do as a Police Procedure, Use of Force, and Wrongful Conviction expert. When I receive the case, discovery, I analyze the case from the genesis of the matter. I analyze the 911 call(s), the station call, citizen contact with patrol officers, patrol officer observations, or any other intervening factors that initiated the sequence of events that caused police involvement. These initial contacts are critical to the case that is being litigated and will have probative value in some instances to the outcome of the case. Let me provide an example.

I was recently retained on a case involving a gang enforcement detail observation that resulted in arresting the alleged suspect for being in possession of a firearm that was in his vehicle. There were three gang enforcement officers in one marked police vehicle. Their probable cause for engaging the suspect was because they smelled a strong odor of marijuana in the vehicle coupled with him being double parked. In reading their written report, their probable cause to engage the suspect due to the strong smell of marijuana was problematic. How could they smell marijuana coming from the car when they were in the process of driving up to the suspect's vehicle? If the probable cause is faulty, everything that proceeds from there may be subject to being inadmissible in court.

In my analysis of the case, I found there was no evidence in the vehicle that suggested the suspect and companion were smoking marijuana. My analysis destroyed their probable cause. I then analyzed the search of the suspect's vehicle by these gang officers where they found an unloaded gun in a closed bag and marijuana in a sealed glass jar. I opined that the search was illegal due to no search warrant or a signed consent to search. I found other issues in this matter, but these were the two major issues. I wrote a detailed expert report outlining my findings. The suspect/defendant was offered a misdemeanor trespass and the underlying charges were dropped.

In analysis in use of force cases, it is critical to ascertain if the force used was reasonable and necessary. In officer involved shootings, policy dictates the use of deadly force is the last option. Administrative guidelines in law enforcement agencies dictate a reverence for life. This is not unique to one or a few law enforcement agencies, but to all law enforcement agencies across the country.

Many experts in my field wrongly testify in court and in their written reports that Peace Officer Standards and Training (POST) are the written guidelines to which agencies adhere to. POST is the regulatory body that certifies law enforcement training of local law enforcement agencies. In POST learning domains, they instruct the student to follow the policies and procedures of the law enforcement agency that has hired them. POST learning domains drives policy, it is not policy. As an example, POST teaches the use of a carotid hold in its Use of Force learning domain. County Council to a certain law enforcement agency has prohibited the use of the carotid hold due to risk management issues. Thus an example of POST driving policy but not being policy.

In Wrongful Conviction cases, as I will discuss later in this book, as well as Police Procedure and Use of Force cases, there are underlying foundations that are critical for successful study and analysis in these areas. To be a competent expert in my areas of expertise you must have patrol experience, staying current with patrol procedures. Second, you must have a thorough knowledge of tactics, use of force application, de-escalation tactics and how they should be implemented in certain situations. Last and most important, a broad and in-depth investigative background. Without that in-depth investigative background, key and critical information to the case an expert is analyzing can and will be missed. Certain reports that are needed and missing from the file will not be requested due to lack of investigative experience. As I further discuss these issues in this book, these needed qualifications will become clearer.

Expert work in my field of expertise requires extensive study, research, and analysis, which is very time consuming. It requires above average written and oral communicative skills, attention to detail and a detailed knowledge of investigations, both criminal and civil. As the reader takes this journey, the required skill sets as outlined will become obvious.

CHAPTER 2

DISCOVERY ISSUES

THE DISCOVERY PROCESS is a critical step in both criminal and civil investigations. Discovery is the obtaining of police reports, scientific reports, administrative reports, policy and procedure, or any documents needed for litigation in a civil or criminal case. As an expert, one should assist retaining counsel in requesting the proper discovery that will be needed in putting on an effective case. In civil rights cases, there is a discovery cutoff date where additional discovery cannot be requested. The problem I have experienced in some civil rights cases I have worked on, the cutoff for discovery preceded my involvement in the case. I have found in a few of those cases that after my review and analysis, certain discovery that was needed was not obtained. When I lecture before attorneys I always suggest they engage their experts early in the case, and long before the close of discovery in the civil rights cases.

An expert must know what type of discovery to ask for that will assist the retaining counsel in putting on an effective case. In a civil rights case I was retained on, there was an issue as to a rear license plate illumination. The officer stated he stopped the vehicle in question because the rear license plate light was not working. I requested through retaining counsel any and all forensic analysis that was completed on the rear license plate light. The discovery requested was received, and it showed the rear license plate light was in fact working at the time of the vehicle stop. In that particular case, I was retained before the discovery cutoff. If I was retained after the discovery cutoff, that critical bit of information would have not been obtained.

In a criminal case I was retained on, the defendant was alleged to have shot at two individuals inside of a residence, missing both victims. The defendant was alleged to have had the gun on his person, prior to the shooting. As an expert, and one who has conducted hundreds of criminal investigations, I knew the allegations in this shooting must be corroborated through a concise and thorough criminal investigation. I requested through defense counsel specific forensic analysis results that should have been completed (discovery), and found the required analysis was not done. My analysis of the discovery and the lack of a required crime scene investigation by the assigned law enforcement patrol and detective personnel showed nothing was done to corroborate the defendant had custody and control of a gun.

Further, there were conflicting versions by the victims as to the alleged shooting that were not rectified by a thorough and concise criminal investigation. Compounded by an incompetent investigation that fell below law enforcement standards, the district attorney's office still filed criminal charges against the defendant. The defendant was facing life in prison on what I found to be a botched and incompetent investigation. I wrote a detailed expert report outlining my findings based on law enforcement standards and the violation of policy and procedures by the detective personnel involving the law enforcement agency that was responsible for the investigation of this case. I testified as an expert in this case, and the defendant was found not guilty.

Wrongful conviction cases require a critical eye for detail, longevity, depth in investigative experience, and a history of historical forensic and investigative analysis. Wrongful conviction cases can range from five to thirty years in wrongful incarceration. In these types of cases, the right type of discovery is critical. The requested discovery must have historical relevance to the case at the time of the case conception, and the expert must know what to ask for. Training records for detective and patrol personnel are critical and must have the historical perspective as it relates to discovery requests. An expert must have the historical experience to know what policy and procedures, manuals of a specific nature, and training documentation to ask for.

In one of my wrongful conviction cases, the plaintiff spent approximately 25 years in prison for a murder he did not commit. The discovery process in this case was a deep dive which resulted in me receiving twelve bank boxes of discovery. I wrote a fifty-plus page expert report on my findings and the discovery I reviewed and analyzed. My expert report was based upon policy and procedure in place in the concerned law enforcement agency at the time of the incident.

The opposing expert on the case wrote a report on policy and procedure that was in place at the time the report was written. There was no reference in the opposing expert's report as to policy and procedure at the time of the incident. In reviewing the opposing expert's Curriculum Vitae, they had no investigative experience during their law enforcement career and no continuing education post-law enforcement retirement. The case settled on my expert report and the plaintiff received a substantial compensation for his wrongful conviction and wrongful incarceration.

Use of force cases require a critical eye for tactics, analysis of the concerned agencies policies and procedures, and law enforcement standards as it relates to use of force. I have analyzed use of force cases in different parts of the country, and the policies are pretty much the same.

I handled one use of force case where the concerned department forbid the use of the carotid hold. As an expert in a use of force case, the analysis has to focus on the written documentation of the force the officer used, to the injuries the defendant/plaintiff received. The question that must be asked, "Are the injuries consistent to the officer's written report?"

In one of the use of force cases I was retained on, the defendant was alleged to fit the description of a robbery suspect and was forcibly taken into custody. I requested through defense counsel the robbery report the defendant was allegedly connected to. In my review and analysis of the robbery report, the defendant did not fit the description of the alleged suspect. The suspect in the robbery report did not have any visible tattoos, and the defendant that was taken into custody had tattoos all over his face.

At the time of the defendant's arrest, crime scene photos showed a lot of blood on the sidewalk at the site of the arrest. During the course of discovery, I was given a copy of security video that captured the arrest and use of force the defendant sustained. I suggested to defense counsel they retain my audio-video expert I utilize on my cases, and requested the security video be enhanced.

Upon the video enhancement, it showed the defendant being kicked in the face twice by one of the arresting officers. The enhanced video corroborated why the presence of the blood was on the sidewalk at the scene of the arrest. This wrongful arrest was further compounded by the district attorney filing robbery charges against the wrong suspect. I wrote a detailed expert report outlining my findings. My report resulted in the case being dismissed. Without the proper analysis that was introduced into this case, the defendant could have been wrongfully convicted for a crime he did not commit, which would have resulted in him spending many years wrongfully incarcerated.

CHAPTER 3

WRITTEN REPORTS

THOROUGH AND CONCISE written expert reports are critical to the success of both criminal and civil rights cases in the area of police procedures, use of force, and wrongful convictions matters. The author of an expert report does not know where that report will ultimately land in the judicial system. In my opinion, the expert report is reflective of the competency, expertise, and knowledge of the expert. For this to be experienced, training in the art of expert report writing is a must.

Experts transition from their respective fields that are the foundation for their areas of expertise to the field of expert work. There is a difference in written communication in one's profession. Writing in an individual's area of discipline, in the narrative that is unique to that discipline, is different than writing an expert report that may be viewed by individuals who are not the expert's peers and are not steeped in the expert's area of discipline. Writing is an art which requires written communication to different audiences who will understand and comprehend in lay terms what is being communicated, and to the audience of individuals who will make critical decisions on the written expert report.

In my areas of expertise, my written report will be reviewed by my retaining counsel, the opposing counsel(s), the opposing expert, and judge in civil matters. The written report can and will define the expert before the expert is seen or before the expert testifies. If the expert is good in written communication, the expert should be a good oral communicator as well. Conversely, if an expert is not a good written communicator, they more than likely will be an average oral communicator at best.

When I read the opposing expert's deposition transcripts involving the case I am retained on, I define the expert by their written report. Many times, I am up against the same opposing expert I had in prior cases, but I will define them on the specific case before me at the time. In other words, the opposing expert is defined independent of their other cases I have been exposed to. If their expert report is superficial, they come off superficial in their deposition most of the time. If they come across with a strong, well written expert report and their deposition presentation is superficial, it may bring questions as to the authenticity of the written expert report. There should not be a disconnect between the opposing expert written report and the opposing expert deposition.

The meat and the genesis of the expert report reflects the experts' background, education, and experience, which lays the foundation of the individual's qualification of being an expert in their particular area of expertise. The next aspects of the expert report are the documents the expert relied upon for their findings and the summary of the case.

The summary should lay out the critical aspects of the case with specificity. The final aspect of the expert report is the detailed findings of the expert. The findings of the expert report are critical based upon a coherent analysis of the facts of the case. The findings should be chronological in approach, reflecting a detailed analysis based on policy, procedure, and industry standards.

As the expert is developing the findings, the findings must be developed to withstand opposing counsel challenges. A lengthy report does not mean a strong report. The expert's writing skills, analytical skills, comprehension skills, and knowledge base are on display via the expert report. The deep dive analysis of the facts of the case will separate an expert from their peers. A thorough and deep dive expert report can have a direct impact in a criminal matter. It may lead to a reasonable offer for the defendant by the people, or it could lead to a dismissal of all criminal charges. In civil rights cases, it may lead to a structured testimony as defined by the court.

The expert must defend their findings in the deposition arena and in criminal and civil rights trials. In criminal cases, some states do not require a deposition before criminal trial, and some states require deposition before criminal trial if the expert is scheduled to testify at that trial. The findings of the expert must be supported by the concerned law enforcement agency policies and procedures and law enforcement standards. Findings should not reflect what the expert would do, but what applied policy and procedure dictates. Findings should also address training of the involved law enforcement personnel that should have been employed to the situation at hand.

The expert report must embrace the four corners of the discovery that were reviewed and analyzed. The expert should not freelance outside of the received discovery. Sometimes there are critical reports or studies that have been completed and embraced by the law enforcement community. If those studies are referenced in the expert report, they must be applicable to the facts at hand, embraced as industry standards, and submitted as an exhibit to the report.

The report must stay in the lane of the expert. If the expert expounds with scientific specificity on the issue of DNA, and the expert is not a court qualified or qualified DNA expert, and does not have the requisite scientific training and credentials, that portion of the report will more than likely be rendered null and void by opposing counsel and the court. On that same theme, if an expert states in the findings that a DNA analysis should have been requested based on an investigative tool that should have been utilized during the course of the investigation, that finding should withstand the challenge from opposing counsel predicated on the expert's background, education, experience, and continuing education.

As an expert, where I have testified over 200 times in trial and deposition in my practice, I have found when I testify in a court trial in both criminal and civil rights cases, on some of my written findings I may not be allowed to testify about due to opposing counsel challenges and the court rulings on those challenges. Counsel on both sides will argue to keep certain expert findings away from expert trial testimony before the jury. Sometimes those arguments succeed and sometimes they don't. The concerned expert is not in the courtroom when these arguments are heard and decisions made by the court.

CHAPTER 4

CONTINUING EDUCATION AND DON'TS IN REPORT WRITING

IT HAS BEEN my experience that some, not all, opposing experts' findings are not applicable to the case that is before them at the time. One of the glaring issues I have found is not analyzing cases with policy that was in place at the time of the incident, even when the requisite policy was submitted during the discovery process.

One of my main concerns with some opposing experts is the length of their reports. I have seen reports twenty to thirty pages in length, minus exhibits, that say absolutely nothing of substance and may have two or three findings, some of which are not supported by the concerned law enforcement policies or procedures and/or comport with law enforcement industry standards.

Another area of concern is the lack of continuing education. An expert or a person who holds him or herself out as an expert must stay current in their craft through continuing education, which should be documented in their Curriculum Vitae. Some opposing experts have no documented continuing education in the last ten years of their practice. As an expert, my personal standards are twenty to forty hours of continuing education per year. Continuing education is critical in my areas of expertise, in that issues that impact my craft can change overnight, so to speak. As an expert, I must be informed as to science that impacts upon my craft, I must be informed as to case law and new case law that impacts my trial testimony and expert written reports.

In 2017, I was scheduled to testify in a criminal matter, and retaining counsel informed me just before I was to take the stand to testify that my testimony would be impacted by a ruling that came down from the California Supreme Court in People v. Marcos Arturo Sanchez 63 Cal 4th 665 (2016), that has an impact on hearsay and expert witnesses. I was informed my testimony would be based on hypothetical questions on direct. I was somewhat aware of the Sanchez case, as it was discussed in the Los Angeles Daily Journal, Vol. 130 No. 192, dated October 4, 2017.

After my testimony in the criminal matter, I was instrumental in moderating a panel made up of judges, private attorneys, and the district attorney, that discussed and trained myself and other experts on People v. Sanchez and other issues that impacted experts in the courtroom. The daily reading of the Los Angeles Daily Journal keeps me current with legal trends and issues that impact upon my craft.

I am not an attorney and don't pretend to be one, but I believe in staying up on what I should be up on. When I was with the Los Angeles Police Department, I had assignments that received the Los Angeles Daily Journal and developed the habit of reading it every day, which also kept me current in my detective work along with my other law enforcement continuing education. I cannot overemphasize continuing education. A sharp opposing counsel will attempt to challenge an expert on continuing education.

I am contacted from time to time to refer experts in other areas of expertise. If I don't see any continuing education on their Curriculum Vitae, I will not refer. I was a consulting expert on a case, being allowed to sit with counsel during trial. The peoples' expert, who was a sworn law enforcement detective, was testifying in an area that was outdated for sworn law enforcement involvement. I leaned over to counsel and suggested he ask the expert when he was last trained and what continuing education pursuits, he undertook to stay current in his area of his alleged expertise. His answer was, he had no training in the area he was testifying as an expert in, in over twenty years. The judge immediately ruled he was not an expert, his testimony was not allowed, and was asked to step down from the witness stand.

Another concern I have with opposing expert reports is the quoting of case law. I am constantly reading expert reports from opposing experts that read like legal motions, laced with points and authorities. Experts in my area of expertise are not lawyers, and if they were, they should write coherent expert reports and not legal briefs. Experts should not be quoting case law in their reports. The courts can disallow their reports based upon that. The quoting of case law must be left to the attorneys in the case.

Experts should remain in their lane and quote policy, procedure, and law enforcement industry standards. Policy and procedure will itself embrace case law, and as an expert one should know that. Knowledge of case law is a requirement for the development of coherent findings, and if asked in a deposition or trial setting, the expert can orally articulate the legal foundation of their findings, if they are allowed to testify in that manner. In reality, in a trial setting the judge would probably not allow an expert to render legal findings or legal opinions.

CHAPTER 5

CREDIBILITY

AS AN EXPERT in the areas of Police Procedure, Use of Force, and Wrongful Convictions, the majority of my practice is on the plaintiff's side in civil rights cases and the defense side in criminal cases. In wrongful conviction cases, 100% of my practice in that area of expertise is on the side of the plaintiff.

I am always asked about the makeup of the cases I have handled, if they are plaintiff, defense, or prosecution, in my trial and deposition testimony. My response in criminal cases is that I am available to both sides. In reality, the law enforcement agencies have their own cadre of experts and I would not expect to be retained by the prosecution in those cases. On the rare occasion I have been retained by a district attorney's office as a Police Procedure and Use of Force expert on a high-profile case involving a police officer who was being tried for murder, a case in which I testified in. On another rare occasion, I was interviewed by another district attorney's office as a Police Procedure and Use of Force expert in a high-profile case involving police officers who were being tried for murder. I was not retained in that matter. On the civil rights side, I have been retained a few times by attorneys who were representing law enforcement agencies.

Credibility is always foremost on my mind as I accept retention on cases in my areas of expertise. In high profile cases, there are a lot of opinions floating in the media which are further expounded upon by alleged experts on the matter. As an expert, one has to block out the noise of opinion(s) and analyze the case objectively. As an expert, you owe it to the retaining counsel to give them the good, bad, and the ugly of the case so they can competently represent their client. If a theory of the case is at play and expert analyses refutes that theory, the expert must be forthright as to why that theory would not work.

I was retained on a three-defendant attempt murder case where defense counsel theory on a drive-by shooting was not supported by scientific analysis. My analysis of the case showed the on-scene investigation fell below law enforcement standards and was in violation of the concerned law enforcement agencies policies and procedures. Further, there was nothing in the case, based upon my analysis, that connected the defendants to this attempted murder. My analysis did not support the counsel's theory and I could not testify to that. I informed counsel that if I testified as it related to their theory, I would not be a credible expert based upon my background, education, and experience, and I would not testify. After discussion with all counsel they agreed to accept my expert analysis. I testified and outlined in my testimony the investigative procedures that should have been and were not applied. Further, I testified as to the available scientific resources that should have been and were not utilized. Finally, my testimony showed nothing corroborated the defendant's involvement in the attempted murder. As a result of my testimony, the jury found all defendants not guilty.

In depositions and trial testimony, I am asked on a regular basis as to the credibility of the officers, supervisors, and management as it relates to the case at hand. As an expert, my job is to render my opinions, orally and in writing, based upon specific policies and procedures and law enforcement industry standards based upon the issues that are presented in the case. It is not my job, or the job of any expert, to render credibility findings on the parties in the case. Credibility issues are left to the triers of fact, the jury in a trial setting and the judge in a court trial.

I have been asked in civil rights trials by opposing counsel credibility questions as to the defendants involved in the case, and my response is always the credibility issues are left to the decisions of the triers of fact. In criminal cases, I have been asked by prosecutors if I believe the defendant is not guilty. Again, my response to that question is left to the trier of fact.

An expert's credibility is also based upon their dress attire and grooming. The dress attire for depositions should be the same as court trial testimony. This is a form of credibility. Appearance matters, and credibility is established once an expert is presented. I have seen experts in video recorded depositions dressed as if they are going to a baseball or football game. Their presentation is totally unprofessional and does not play well before a jury if portions of the deposition is shown by opposing counsel during jury trial.

When an expert arrives for deposition or trial testimony, hair should be well groomed, if men wear beards the beards should be well groomed, fingernails clean, shoes polished/clean, heals not run over, and men who don't wear a beard should present themselves clean shaven and not look like they need a shave. Men should wear a suit and tie, preferably with a white shirt. Recommended court/deposition colors are black, navy blue, or dark gray. Proper professional appearance is a respect to the jury, respect to and for the court, and it shows the expert as a true professional in their areas of expertise. Female experts should also be well groomed for depositions and trial with the same attention to details as their male counterparts. Again, recommended court deposition colors for women should be business attire black, navy blue, or dark gray with appropriate business attire footwear.

Opposing counsel always asks in the presence of the jury what the expert's hourly rates are, how much they have been paid, and how many hours are left to bill. The expert's dress attire should comport to the fees they demand. Every time I go to court, I dress prepared to testify, whether I testify or not. When I meet with counsel I always dress as though I am going to court to testify.

A few years ago, I was walking down the hall in a court building and was introduced to an attorney by another attorney. After approximately five minutes of discussion,

I walked away with a respectable-sized and agreed upon expert retainer agreement on a high-profile murder case. If I was in jeans, tennis shoes, shirt, and sport coat, I would not have been given the introduction to the attorney or received the retainer or the case. Remember, your reputation will always precede you.

CHAPTER 6

SUPPORTING EXPERTS

AS A DETECTIVE investigating complex criminal investigations while working LAPD, I always utilized scientific experts to assist me in solving cases I was working on. If a gun was used and fired in a crime I was investigating, I consulted with a ballistic expert to assist me in my investigation. If there was an issue with obtaining fingerprints to assist in the apprehension of a suspect or suspects, I would consult with a fingerprint expert to harvest the fingerprints, process, and analyze them. If there was blood work to be analyzed at a crime scene, I would bring those experts in as well. Detectives who investigate criminal investigations will develop theories as to who may be involved in committing the crime or crimes under investigation, and the science or other specified evidence must corroborate a targeted individual's involvement in the crime.

As I transitioned from the prosecution side to the defense side in criminal investigations and the plaintiff side in civil rights cases and wrongful conviction cases, I analyze these cases to see if investigative procedures were utilized to connect the suspects, defendants, and convicted to the crimes they were allegedly arrested and convicted for. I have analyzed over 1,200 cases in my private practice and have found a vast majority of the cases I have worked on to be lacking in involving critical scientific resources to corroborate investigative theories and suspect involvement. These cases I have analyzed have gone from simple to complex in nature. As I brought scientific resources to the cases I investigated when I was working LAPD, I bring those same resources to the cases I analyze in my practice.

Police procedure analysis requires an in-depth knowledge of scientific resources that are utilized in investigations. If there is a gun involved in a case I am analyzing, be it civil or criminal, I will, if applicable, opine as to possible gunshot residue (GSR) either on the clothing, hands, or interior of a vehicle or other relevant objects that would corroborate certain portions of allegations that have been introduced into the case. It will also show if the defendant and or decedent had custody and control of an alleged gun or was in the environment of possible gunfire.

In a lot of cases that I have analyzed, this critical analysis is not done by patrol officers or assigned detective personnel. I will request through retaining counsel the services of a ballistic expert to opine from a scientific perspective what chemical elements would be present if in fact the person of interest or decedent in an officer involved shooting case was in possession and control of a firearm. The same as it relates to trajectory analysis as to shots fired.

Ballistic trajectory analysis is critical when shots are fired by both suspects and law enforcement officers in officer-involved shootings. In one civil rights case involving an officer-involved shooting, with the help of a ballistic expert it was shown the shooting did not occur the way the concerned law enforcement agency stated in their reports.

DNA analysis is just as important. Early in my civil rights work, DNA analysis, for the most part, was not included in the investigations conducted by the officers conducting officer-involved shootings if there was a gun allegedly being used, in some instances, by the decedent.

In my analysis of the shooting, I would opine DNA analysis should have been requested on the weapon in question to confirm the plaintiff or decedent had custody and control of the alleged weapon. If DNA analysis was in fact completed by law enforcement and there was a connection to the decedent, I would suggest to retaining counsel a DNA expert be retained to examine the credibility of the analysis that was done.

I had a criminal case involving law enforcement officers in a life and death fight with a suspect, where it was alleged the suspect grabbed an officer's gun, almost disarming the officer. The suspect was taken into custody without any shots being fired. DNA analysis was completed on both officers' guns. The officer who alleged the suspect took his weapon during the physical altercation did not have the suspect's DNA on his weapon. The partner officer who denied the suspect ever touched his weapon, the suspect's DNA was on that officer's weapon. Bringing in a DNA expert uncovered a problem that would have otherwise been overlooked.

Handwriting analysis is critical in some criminal cases. This area of investigation is often overlooked. Competent handwriting analysis has excluded individuals from being involved in criminal activity that otherwise would have resulted in wrongful convictions. During my law enforcement experience, I have utilized the services of handwriting experts to connect and exclude suspect involvement in the criminal matters I was investigating. I have utilized the same resource in my private practice, and through retaining counsel I have utilized the services of handwriting experts in cases I have analyzed.

As a police procedure expert, I could not do what I do without bringing in subject matter experts in specific scientific areas. I call this completed analysis of the case. If there are blood spatter issues you bring in a blood spatter expert to tell you what you have and if it lines up with the law enforcement investigation. Blood spatter tells a story of how certain events occurred and possible physical evidence that may manifest itself.

I was retained on a murder case involving a double homicide involving the usage of a shotgun in a confined room. There was blood spatter all over the room to include walls and partial ceiling. The suspect turned himself into the police the same day of the murders along with the shotgun that was utilized. The suspect's clothing, shoes, and shotgun contained no blood spatter from the victims of this murder.

I convinced retaining counsel to retain the expertise of a blood spatter expert. It was determined the suspect would have blood spatter on his person and the shotgun if they, the defendant, committed the murder. Based upon our analysis, it was determined the suspect, then the defendant made a false confession, which was based on the lack of evidence connecting him to the crime.

CHAPTER 7

MEDIA INTERVIEWS

IT IS MY opinion, as an expert, every time an expert is quoted in print, appears on television, or is interviewed on radio, it's like testifying in court. Every media interview is subject to be revisited in court during an expert's testimony. If an expert testifies in court based upon policy and procedures that are based upon issues in the case and comes across differently in media interviews, playing to public sentiment or advocacy, the expert's credibility will come into question.

If an expert is a repeat media source, opposing counsel will utilize those interviews, both recent and historical, to try to discredit the expert in both deposition and trial settings. In trial settings, the introduction of prior media interviews by the concerned expert to the sitting jury is subject to court rulings. As an expert who is an active source to the media, on television, radio, and in print, in the areas of police procedure, use of force, and wrongful convictions, I try to be fluent with my body of media work to ensure opposing counsel is addressing my media comments in the context in which I gave them. Opposing counsel will attempt to take my interviews out of context to meet their case strategy needs, and I must keep my words in context as I gave them based upon the involved agencies policy, procedure, and law enforcement industry standards.

As an expert, when I am asked to be interviewed on a particular matter as it relates to law enforcement, I will not be interviewed until I am well-versed on the subject matter and have read the printed media coverage and watched the video or prior television coverage on the issue at hand. I have heard and watched my share of alleged police procedure experts, use of force experts, and experts talking about wrongful convictions who are not prepared when interviewed in these areas. Further, there are alleged experts who have not seen the inside of a courtroom , a deposition conference room, or testified in my areas of expertise in years, if at all. There are those that hold themselves as experts in law enforcement issues who have never had law enforcement training or been a sworn law enforcement officer. Then, there are the retired law enforcement officers who are also perceived as experts in my areas of expertise, whose interviews and comments are a walk down memory lane and not current in their craft.

I am in the courtroom , in both federal and state courts, testifying in my areas of expertise on a regular basis. I am deposed on a regular basis, defending my findings based upon my analysis of cases I have been retained on. I am current in my craft and in my areas of expertise. I am in my office five to six days a week, studying and analyzing police procedure, use of force, and wrongful conviction cases. As they say, I am in the game or master of the game.

Technology is advancing in law enforcement and is being utilized in critical tactical situations. Law enforcement is now utilizing drones in critical situations to embrace officer safety issues and the safety of citizens. As a retired law enforcement officer, I can see the benefit and lives it can save. As a retired law enforcement officer who is a police procedure expert, use of force expert, and wrongful conviction expert, I see concerns and potential liability concerns for law enforcement departments and the municipalities who have embraced drone usage.

The media and the community discussions address the concerns of community privacy issues in usage of drones in the urban setting. It is my opinion there has not been a deep dive discussion in the media as to the legal oversight into drone usage by law enforcement. It is my professional opinion that the usage of drones by law enforcement should have judicial oversight and be treated the same as obtaining a search warrant to conduct a search of a residence or other containments which require a search warrant.

The media is a powerful educational tool for the public. To be effective, subject matter experts must be current in their craft and provide a deep dive analysis. In my areas of expertise, you rarely hear the deep dive investigative analysis as it relates to police procedure, use of force, and wrongful conviction issues. There is boilerplate language that has been adopted by law enforcement agencies all across the country to justify what is done as it relates to use of force issues that you rarely hear about in media interviews. There is boilerplate language you hear that is on audio from body cameras that officers wear and documented in police reports that you rarely hear about in media interviews. There is boilerplate language in officer involved shootings that is used across the country that you read in officer involved shooting reports that you rarely hear about in media interviews. There are investigative issues I address and challenge in police procedure, use of force, and wrongful conviction cases that are rarely talked about in media interviews by other alleged experts in my field. The chain of command and its involvement during an event, the chain of command involvement post event, and the chain of command involvement in the investigative phase are other areas that are rarely discussed in media interviews.

When I am interviewed by the media on high profile law enforcement events, I try to give an interview that not only deals with policy, procedure, and law enforcement industry standards, but take the interview into a deep dive investigative analysis, discussing resources that should be brought into the situation at hand.

In my media interviews, I discuss the issue of corroboration that is critical on the investigative side. I discuss the corroboration of officers' statements that is a critical investigative process. I discuss the corroboration of witness statements that is a critical investigative process. In my media interviews, I discuss the issue of thorough alibi investigations, which is a critical investigative step and a step that is missing in most wrongful conviction cases. The media interview must embrace a complete analysis of the event to include the investigative side, which is most often absent from the media interviews.

CHAPTER 8

AN INFORMED APPROACH TO USE OF FORCE AND THE BENCH

ON OCCASION, WHEN I am a testifying expert on a matter I am retained on, with the court's permission, I get a chance to sit in on trial testimony of opposing police procedure experts and sworn officers involved in the case. I am amazed in some testimony that I hear from sworn personnel, in that it has no semblance of coherent policy and procedure. It is painfully clear that the testifying officers are not current with their respective agencies policies and procedures relating to the issues that are before the court and jury, and are not current with law enforcement industry standards.

In reality, the policies and procedures that the respective agency dictates are police policies that are germane to law enforcement agencies across the country and are law enforcement industry standards. These policies are dictated by case law and not applied to any certain agency, but applied to all law enforcement agencies across the country. There are multi-jurisdictional task forces with sworn law enforcement personnel from different law enforcement agencies working together on certain criminal activity issues. They all operate under the same policies and are trained the same way, respective of agency. In some instances, there are sworn federal law enforcement officers embedded in the multi-jurisdictional task forces.

I testify in different jurisdictions across the country and have been deemed an expert in every jurisdiction I have testified in. I have been challenged by opposing counsel that I have only worked the Los Angeles Police Department and have not been exposed to the respective agency I am testifying about. I then explain through testimony that law enforcement policies are harmonious regardless of agency, but may vary as to procedures. Some agencies' policies are more restrictive than other agencies due to risk management exposure.

I have found much of expert testimony and expert report writing are what I call traditional testimony and traditional expert report writing. A few experts in my field study and are current in their craft, and others lean on their experience which is based on law enforcement traditions which can cut corners and do not embrace coherent policy.

The problem with this traditional testimony and traditional expert report writing, the bench hears this type of testimony on a regular basis and may accept the traditional expert finding as factual. I had a situation where a federal judge had heard about my position on Peace Officer Standards and Training (POST) learning domains, and requested my testimony under oath on the issue. I testified that the POST learning domains are not law enforcement agency policy, but that they drive agency policy. The traditional testimony and expert report writing by experts in my field opine that POST learning domains are law enforcement agency policy.

Opposing counsel obtained a rebuttal witness from the local law enforcement training division to refute my testimony. The rebuttal witness agreed with my testimony and testified that POST learning domains drive law enforcement policy. California POST Learning Domain No. 20, which covers use of force, admonishes that "Peace officers are responsible for becoming familiar with and complying with their agency's policies and guidelines regarding the use of force" (1-7). California POST Learning Domain No. 20 further states, "Limitations on the use of force are set by specific agency policy. All such policies are attempts to provide rational guidelines and to protect the officer and agency from criminal and civil liability" (1-9).

These POST learning domain admonishments support the position that the POST learning domains drive local law enforcement policy and not law enforcement policy. It is important the bench be aware of how POST learning domains are integrated into local law enforcement agency policy, more specifically into the area of use of force.

Another area that is before the court is the issue of suspect resisting. U. S. Department of Justice, Office of Justice Programs, National Institute of Justice, National Law Enforcement Technology Center, published an article in June 1995, "Positional Asphyxia-Sudden Death."

Embedded in that article is "Basic Physiology of a Struggle." The embedded section states in part, "A person lying on his stomach has trouble breathing when pressure is applied on his back. The remedy seems relatively simple: get the pressure off his back. However, during the violent struggle between an officer or officers and a suspect, the solution is not as simple as it may sound. Often, the situation is compounded by a vicious cycle of suspect resistance and officer restraint:

- A suspect is restrained in a face-down position, and breathing may become labored.
- Weight is applied to the person's back—the more weight, the more severe the degree of compression.
- The individual experiences increased difficulty breathing.
- The natural reaction to oxygen deficiency occurs—the person struggles more violently.
- The officer applies more compression to subdue the individual."

As I have analyzed many uses of force cases where the defendant in criminal matters and the plaintiff in civil rights matters are accused of resisting, I have found the defendant/plaintiff had three to five officers on his or her back while he or she is yelling, "I can't breathe!" The defendant/plaintiff is experiencing in the area of 700-900 pounds on their back, causing them to struggle to breathe. Based upon my background, education, and experience, I have opined that the individual is not resisting the officers, but is struggling to breathe.

The courts must be aware of this physiological phenomenon that in a majority of the cases where officers are on the back of a defendant or plaintiff, they are not resisting the officers but struggling to breathe. All sworn law enforcement personnel who have gone through a reputable police academy, both federal and local law enforcement training academies, have experienced the weight of individuals on their back and how it restricts breathing.

Use of force is a major law enforcement concern and community concern throughout the country. There are experts in my field who will justify even the most egregious use of force, couching their findings in the traditional testimony and the traditional expert report. Proper study, research, and continuing education will result in coherent and reliable trial testimony and expert reports and a more educated community on this topic.

CHAPTER 9

DON'T STIPULATE, EXAMINE AND ANALYZE EVERYTHING

WITH CLOSE TO five decades of working in the criminal justice system, with over four decades of investigating and analyzing criminal, administrative, and civil investigations, I have developed an approach and advice to retaining defense counsel which is mirrored in my lectures to attorneys. I strongly, and I mean very strongly, suggest to criminal defense counsel, never, never stipulate to anything of an evidentiary nature. Further, never, never stipulate to anything of an investigative nature.

In my seventeen years in private practice where I have focused on police procedure issues, use of force issues, and wrongful conviction issues, where I have analyzed over 1,200 documented cases from different law enforcement agencies across the country, I have found egregious investigative deficiencies and scientific deficiencies that would have led and have led to wrongful convictions.

In the civil rights cases I have handled, which includes a discrimination case against a law enforcement agency, I have seen failures in the concerned law enforcement agencies to ensure proper investigative procedures were adhered to, failures of the law enforcement agencies supervisory and management personnel to ensure polices were followed, and these failures have cost municipalities millions of dollars. I have found through my analysis of hundreds of cases, that a lot of detective personnel are deficient in investigative experience, even those working high profile investigative assignments.

A lawyer without in-depth investigative experience would miss the obvious. As an example, I was retained by defense counsel involving a cold case home invasion murder that was investigated by an elite law enforcement investigative unit. In the pre-trial discovery meeting where the deputy district attorney was present along with the investigating officer, it was very clear to me the detective did not have in-depth investigative experience, which is a critical requirement for the case they were assigned and the division they were working.

With my in-depth investigative background, I did a deep dive analysis of the discovery to include crime scene photographs. In my analysis of the crime scene photographs, I opined the crime scene was staged and appeared to look sexual in nature. The point of entry where the alleged suspect(s) entered the residence failed to show evidence that would support the location as being the point of entry. I testified during the trial as to my findings of the crime scene and point of entry being staged and the investigative reasons why. Along with my testimony and other exculpatory findings during the course of the trial, the jury found the defendant not guilty.

I was informed by retaining counsel the jury deliberated less than an hour. If the defense counsel had stipulated to any investigative findings and not retained my services to assist in the case, the defendant would have been found guilty and spent the rest of his life in prison on a wrongful conviction for a crime he did not commit.

In another matter, I was retained as an expert in a gang drive-by shooting murder. The gun allegedly used in this murder was recovered and it was alleged that the defendant's DNA was found on the murder weapon. On the surface, it appeared to be a slam dunk case for the prosecution. There were some investigative issues I found during my analysis of the case, but they were not strong enough to overcome the defendants DNA on the murder weapon.

I encouraged the retaining counsel to not stipulate to the DNA findings in the case and to request the court to appoint a DNA expert to analyze the peoples' findings in that area. The court granted the request, and a DNA expert was ushered into the case for the defendant, to analyze the DNA findings.

During the subsequent defense meeting, I suggested a deep dive DNA discovery request be completed. As a result of the discovery request and received discovery, the DNA expert found problems with the DNA exam charts, electropherograms, opining they did not support findings linking the DNA to the defendant. Further, it was found the specimen in the case was mixed up with other unrelated specimens.

The DNA expert testified to these findings during the murder trial, along with my testimony of investigative concerns. The jury found the defendant not guilty of murder. If the defense counsel had stipulated to the DNA test of the people, the defendant would have spent the rest of his life in prison for a crime he did not commit. Examining and analyzing the DNA findings set forth by the prosecution, showing the DNA findings did not link the defendant to the DNA, prevented a wrongful conviction for a crime the defendant did not commit.

In the cases I am retained on in the areas of police procedure, use of force, and wrongful convictions, I have observed glaring and subtle errors in investigations that are linked to the lack of investigative experience and training. Further, these errors are compounded by a lack of coherent supervision and poor to non-existent management oversight to the criminal investigations. Management just signing off on the case without in-depth analysis of the investigation is a prevalent occurrence in criminal investigations.

In some very high-profile cases, in my analysis I see management's hands all over the investigation. Management, who in most instances has no credible investigative experience, leads to errors in the investigation. I see shortcuts that are supported by supervision and management to obtain a clearance of the crime by an arrest that in some instances should have never been made. I have seen these problems up close and personal during my close to three decades of investigative experience working as a sworn law enforcement detective.

There are a lot of good and outstanding detective personnel in law enforcement, but there is a group of detective personnel who have embraced shortcuts as it relates to experience with the shortcut approach metastasizing itself through the chain of command, thus exposing itself as incompetence throughout the organization, thus making good and competent detective personnel look bad.

The arresting of an individual is a very powerful responsibility for law enforcement personnel. Equally powerful is the conviction of an individual. At both junctions, arrest and conviction, everyone involved, law enforcement, prosecution, and defense, must do their utmost to get it right. In my close to five decades in this business, the criminal justice system has fallen short. Based upon my lengthy investigative and criminal justice experience, knowing intimately the problems in the criminal justice system to include very poor supervision and very poor management oversight as it relates to true criminal justice, I again strongly encourage defense counsel not stipulate to evidentiary and investigative issues. Defense counsel must independently examine and question everything, leaving no stones unturned.

CHAPTER 10

DEPOSITION AND TRIAL PREPARATION AND TESTIMONY

I HAVE HAD EXTENSIVE training in testifying in court during my Los Angeles Police Department career, and have testified hundreds of times during my law enforcement career in both administrative and criminal matters. In my expert practice, I have testified over two hundred times, which includes trial and deposition testimony.

With all of the testimony experience I have, every time I am sworn in and take the witness stand I take the stand as though that is the first testimony of my career. After I testify as to my credentials supporting my expertise, I then mentally transition to the issues I am there to testify about. I look at testifying as teaching a class that is based on the facts of the case that fall within my areas of expertise that I have been asked to teach the jury about. As I testify, I am studying opposing counsel, and assessing their knowledge based on what I am being questioned on.

After the second or third question, I know if they have an in-depth knowledge of my craft or if they are just trying to be theatrical and play to the jury. Heaven forbid if there is a television camera in the court, then "Oscar performances" are at play. Opposing counsel, in criminal matters which are prosecutors from the city attorney and district attorney's office and in civil rights matters opposing counsel from the city attorney and county counsel office, are surrounded by law enforcement because that is who they represent in civil matters and work with in criminal matters.

I can easily tell who is prepared and who is a legal law enforcement groupie, and so can the jury. They come across as more police than the police. There are opposing counsel that are professional, prepared, and outstanding attorneys who I enjoy going up against. They are very talented attorneys, and I have my opposing counsel favorites, which I keep private and to myself. Then there are opposing counsel who have missed their calling and should have joined law enforcement or some other criminal justice endeavor, which I also keep private and to myself. My observations are based upon almost five decades of courtroom experience.

When I am in preparation for deposition testimony, I have a different preparation regimen than I do for trial testimony preparation. In deposition, your statement are given under oath as it is in court or trial testimony. The difference is, in deposition testimony there is no judge present to prevent certain questioning due to court rulings, so everything is thrown at the expert. As an expert, you must support and defend your report and findings in the deposition setting. I study and know the four corners of the file I received during discovery. I have done my research and supported my findings on the concerned law enforcement agency policy and procedure coupled with law enforcement standards. I get up at 3:00 AM most mornings and arrive in my office between 5-6:00 AM to study and write if a report is due. I am always prepared for trial and deposition testimony. In deposition, I am able to tell if opposing counsel is prepared to challenge me on my findings. I am also able to tell if they are strategizing my deposition for their trial cross-examination of me.

In my trial preparation, I focus on being disciplined in my work and my lifestyle to my work. Clients' freedom are at play in my criminal work and millions of dollars may be at play in my civil rights work. As an expert in police procedure, use of force, and wrongful convictions, my role is a part of a whole. Sometimes, depending upon the case, I may have a small, medium, or large role in the case. Be it large or small, I try to always be ready and prepared for whatever may come my way, be it direct or cross-examination in trial and in deposition. Many years ago, I adopted an edict that states, "Stay Ready to Keep from Getting Ready." This is something I try to embrace in my life endeavors as it relates to my goals, objectives, and work.

In my lectures, when I lecture on deposition and trial testimony preparation, I always bring in the five P's:

Proper

Preparation

Prevents

Poor

Performance

Proper preparation is critical to an expert's deposition and trial testimony. If an expert is not current in their craft, not knowing what type of discovery to request through retaining counsel that is germane to the case at hand and not doing meaningful and relevant study on the case, the expert will have a poor performance in deposition and trial testimony. If an expert does not know their case, all the trial and deposition preparation with retaining counsel will be a waste of time and the expert's career will be short lived.

Opposing counsel will sometimes use strategy in an attempt to trip an expert up, make the expert look bad, or attack the expert's character. If the expert comes across as credible, knows the case and their craft, it will make opposing counsel look very bad in the eyes of the jury. If the expert is not credible, does not know the case or their craft, the expert will look very bad in the eyes of a jury.

When I mentor new experts, I strongly advise them not to testify for the money. In other words. expert testimony must be ethical and not just geared to retaining counsel's strategy. If an expert knows that a trial strategy would compromise the integrity of their testimony, that should be discussed before the expert is on the stand and testifying. You do not want to blindside the retaining counsel. The expert testimony must not go against industry standards and established policy and procedures to embrace a strategy that will make both the expert and retaining counsel look bad. The expert must remember that they are the subject matter expert and work with the retaining counsel for a positive and ethical outcome.

CHAPTER 11

THE PROBLEM—SUPERVISION, MANAGEMENT, AND INTERNAL AFFAIRS

ALL CRIMINAL CASES embrace police procedure issues. The question to be asked, were the police procedure issues followed by the officers and detectives or were the police procedure issues violated by the officers and detectives?

The evaluation must be made not on the traditional approach to law enforcement, but based on policies and procedures of the concerned law enforcement agency. In my analysis of cases, I not only focus on the first responder approach, but also on the supervision approach, the mid-management approach, and the management approach, in both patrol and investigative arenas.

In other words, I analyze how the chain of command addressed the issues that are before me. In criminal cases, I do not see an aggressive approach by defense council past the patrol officers, which are the first responders. There is always a supervision component to all criminal cases, both patrol supervision and detective supervision. There is always a mid-management component to all criminal cases, both patrol mid-management and detective mid-management levels. There is always a management component to all criminal cases for both patrol and detectives. There is always a staff component to all criminal cases for both patrol and detectives.

I have found in my analysis in criminal matters, for the most part, supervision, mid-management, management, and staff sign-off, in some instances, on very bad police work. I call it rubber stamping mediocre and poor work. Defense counsel should aggressively approach the chain of command, in their case in chief, and have them testify as to their approval of questionable to bad police work.

In high profile cases, the chain of command has testified as to their signing off on questionable work. I had one case where I suggested to defense counsel that the concerned agency chief of police come to court and testify as to his allowing questionable to bad police work to make its way into a criminal investigation. The concerned agency chief's office called and stated the chief will not accept the defense subpoena and will not be in court to testify. The defense counsel informed the court of the response given to the defense subpoena, at which time the court called the chief's office, informing the office the chief had thirty minutes to respond to the court or there will be a body attachment for his arrest. The chief responded to the court in ten minutes.

In the civil rights cases I have analyzed, in some instances, all the players in the chain of command are not included in the lawsuit. In some instances, upon my review and analysis of the case, a major player has been identified by my analysis and not included in the lawsuit, and was too late to bring them in. That is why plaintiff counsel in civil rights cases should bring in police procedure experts early into the case, to ensure all required law enforcement personnel are in the lawsuit.

In civil rights lawsuits involving internal affairs investigations, internal affairs investigators assigned to the case along with the entire internal affairs investigators chain of command, must be included in the lawsuit.

I have analyzed internal affairs investigations in civil rights cases from different agencies from different parts of the country, and there is a commonality to all of them. They rubber stamp and will not go against the findings, even when the law enforcement findings are wrong. The majority of internal affairs investigations lack personnel with requisite investigative skills or investigative background, which includes the internal affairs chain of command, who approve some very bad investigations.

I had one case where the internal affairs investigator put in writing that they did not know what a homicide or murder book was. It was determined that the internal affairs investigator never worked homicide or any criminal investigative assignment. If the investigator found what a homicide book was, they would not know what to do with it once they found it.

I had another civil rights case, involving a sexual abuse investigation. The internal affairs investigator put in writing that they had to read a book to learn how to address a sexual assault investigation. The investigators chain of command approved their botched investigation. It was determined through deposition that the internal affairs investigators never worked a criminal investigative assignment.

The problem with internal affairs and staffing that assignment with qualified investigative personnel is a systemic problem nationwide. Internal affairs assignments have been looked at as coveted assignments geared for upward mobility. This approach has cost and will continue to cost municipalities millions of dollars in civil rights lawsuits.

A close analysis of internal affairs investigations is critical in civil rights investigations. If the case is subject to a civil lawsuit, the internal affairs investigation will more than likely rubber stamp the theme of the law enforcement case. They will not drill down into the investigative analysis of the case due to their lack of investigative knowledge.

The majority of law enforcement agencies across the country are patrol oriented with a very quiet focus on investigations. Until the law enforcement community has an aggressive duality approach, embracing patrol and investigations equally as a focus of upward mobility, there will be a continued problem with internal affairs investigations.

Internal affairs investigations are critical in identifying internal problems within the organization, be it patrol issues, detective issues, or management and staff issues. Coherent internal affairs investigations are designed to identify organizational problems, and that will lead in a direction that will correct systems that are a liability to the organization. When internal affairs becomes the problem, and the impediment to and for needed organizational change, then the law enforcement organization will be consistently faced with civil litigation.

Not only is the issue of internal affairs a systemic issue, it is an issue of competent leadership. Having worked in and around law enforcement almost all of my adult life, change is almost non-existent without judicial intervention, which in most cases is federal judicial intervention in the form of consent decrees. Law enforcement leadership will probably disagree with my take on internal affairs and its personnel makeup, and that is alright. The disagreement just confirms the leadership problem that is so prevalent in law enforcement and the criminal justice community. Change is hard for any organization and almost impossible for law enforcement organizations. Law enforcement staff and management have to learn to put square pegs in square holes instead of putting round pegs in square holes. Doing the same thing over and over again and expecting change is the definition of insanity.

CHAPTER 12

MY CRIMINAL JUSTICE PERSPECTIVE

IN MY PRIVATE practice, I have had to take the thirty-five-thousand-foot view of the criminal justice system. National discussion has intimated the criminal justice system is broken and not working. In some instances, I have seen the system work and justice achieved. In other instances, I have seen justice denied. In some instances, I have seen the criminal justice system fail miserably with no concern as to who was harmed in the process. I have seen lives ruined in taking a deal for crimes they did not commit due to not trusting the system to allow them their due process as it relates to a fair trial, or not wanting continued incarceration while awaiting trial. I have seen the system work more harshly in minority communities than in White communities.

I was testifying in a criminal trial as a police procedure expert in a matter I was retained on, and a young deputy district attorney asked me, in front of a jury, if policing was different in minority communities or the same in all communities. The deputy district attorney made the mistake of asking a question of a testifying expert witness not knowing what the answer would be. My answer was that policing is different and more aggressive in minority communities than it is in White communities. I testified that I have worked in both communities as a patrol officer and as a detective, and there is a difference in policing in those respective communities. I further testified that there is a Rodeo Drive (now Barack Obama Boulevard) in the Black community in Los Angeles, and there is a Rodeo Drive (not a Barack Obama Boulevard) in Beverly Hills. The policing on both of the Rodeo Drives are polar opposites. Policing should be the same in all communities, but in reality, and sadly, it is not.

In that case, the jury listened to all the testimony, due process was experienced, justice was served, and the defendant was found not guilty. From my perspective, the criminal justice system is not broken, but it is on life support. If individuals are spending decades in prison for crimes they did not commit, the system is not working and is broken for them. If policing is different and harsher in minority communities than in White communities, the system is not working and is broken in the minority communities. If individuals are taking deals in court for crimes they did not commit and not believing they will receive justice if they go to trial, the system is not working and is broken for them.

What I handle in my practice is not even the tip of the iceberg. I receive calls from all over the country with people desperately in search for help in trying to acquire justice and fair treatment in their cases. I receive calls from individuals who allege wrongful convictions after decades of incarceration and are seeking help. I receive calls from individuals who allege they were the recipients of police beatings seeking help. I have been interviewed by media outlets locally and from across the country on video documented egregious police use of force and very questionable police shootings. The system is not working, and at this point in time I see nothing in place or on the horizon to turn this system, that is on life support, around.

I have been working in the criminal justice system since 1974. When I started, there was a civility between opposing counsel and law enforcement and defense counsel. There was also civility and respect for the bench. Over the decades, that civility, for the most part, has eroded and is absent. I have seen opposing counsel which includes prosecution at each other's throat in criminal matters, in front of the public.

I have seen both defense and prosecution show little or no respect for the bench, in front of the public. Mind you, this is not the norm, but when the public observes this they believe this goes on in all courtrooms. There is a posture of arrogance by a few new and seasoned prosecutors that I have seen locally and across the country that does not go unnoticed by the public. This arrogance erodes trust in the system and lends itself to unintended outcomes and civil liability as it relates to wrongful convictions. The majority of attorneys, both defense and prosecution, and plaintiff in my orbit are highly professional, non-adversarial and seasoned. The reality is, the failures of a few impact the view of the majority.

Finally, I have seen problems in the screening of criminal matters by the prosecutor's office both locally, regionally, and nationally as to the filing of criminal cases. During my tenure in law enforcement, the filing deputy district attorney and the filing deputy city attorney would scrutinize every aspect of the case and not hesitate in not filing the case if the investigation did not meet prosecutorial standards. Some of the criminal cases I have cited in this book would have never been filed under the prosecutorial guidelines I and other investigators were exposed to during my law enforcement career. The problem does not only fall as a prosecutorial problem, but also a law enforcement supervisory problem.

Detective supervisors must review all cases prior to those cases being submitted to the prosecution for filing. This is the form of checks and balances. The goal is thoroughness in the investigative aspect of the case, thoroughness in the prosecutorial filing of the case, and due process and justice experienced by the defendant in all aspects in the litigation of the criminal matter before the court and jury.

When due process and justice is experienced, be it guilty, not guilty, or a hung jury decision, trust in the system will begin to be embraced by all citizens and communities in this country. There will be progress in the prosecutorial process, where those that are charged will feel they will get a fair shake by going through the trial system and not feel they would need to take a deal for something they did not do, due to the lack of trust in the system.

All aspects of the criminal justice system should be subjected to meaningful self-examination and external examination for correction, improvement which will embrace due process, and justice in a more holistic manner.

Made in the USA
San Bernardino, CA
27 March 2020